Fun Curriculum Activities (K-6) for Teachers and Media Specialists

Fast, Easy & Cheap!

Sue Stidham

The Scarecrow Press, Inc.
Lanham, Maryland, and London
2003

SCARECROW PRESS, INC.

Published in the United States of America
by Scarecrow Press, Inc.
A Member of the Rowman & Littlefield Publishing Group
4501 Forbes Boulevard, Suite 200, Lanham, Maryland 20706
www.scarecrowpress.com

PO Box 317
Oxford
OX2 9RU, UK

Layout and interior design by Lisbeth Ohse. Illustrations by Beth Sukraw.

British Library Cataloguing in Publication Information Available

ISBN 0-8108-4673-X (pbk: alk. paper)

♾™The paper used in this publication meets the minimum requirements of
American National Standard for Information Sciences—Permanence of
Paper for Printed Library Materials, ANSI/NISO Z39.48-1992.
Manufactured in the United States of America.

Dedicated to all students, teachers, and media specialists who like to have fun.

Website Information

To access any one of the links listed in the activities in this book, simply go to, or bookmark, the website:

http://www.pittstate.edu/edsc/ssls/fun.html

From here, each activity from the book has a hyperlink to websites that complement and correlate with the activities in the book. Check the site every time you do an activity, since the sites will be constantly up-dated.

Contents

Acknowledgments

A book written by educators for educators cannot be written in isolation. With that in mind, I want to give special thanks to my family at home and at Pitt State, and especially to Lisbeth Ohse and Beth Sukraw, whose tireless efforts and amazing talents saved the day, again and again. I want to also thank all teachers who love kids and books and having fun. To them, I dedicate this book.

Fun Curriculum Activities (K-6) for Teachers and Media Specialists

Introduction

Teachers are often expected to do more with less. Searching through catalogs that offer spectacular resources at high prices is frustrating. Even the most energetic, caring teachers can be tempted to give up. But, offer those same teachers a few fast, easy, and cheap ideas for resources and watch out!

That's the purpose of this book—to offer resources that are simple, fast, and fun. Additional ideas have been included so that a broader range of students can be reached. But, what about those incredible websites that take time to find? Well, they're included. The websites are even linked to the author's home page, so that the online resources are always updated and available.

The simple and logical arrangement of these innovative resources provides quick access for even the busiest teacher or media specialist. The format provides a foolproof listing of needed materials so that even the most basic necessity won't be forgotten. The average cost per project is less than $10.00 per class, and usually far less.

The primary teaching strategy for this book encourages critical thinking, collaboration, problem solving, and experimental learning. The projects are designed to enhance lesson plans for K-6 students, and many are designed to reinforce computer skills.

Absolutely Abstract

MATERIALS

1. WHITE PAPER
2. TEMPERA PAINTS

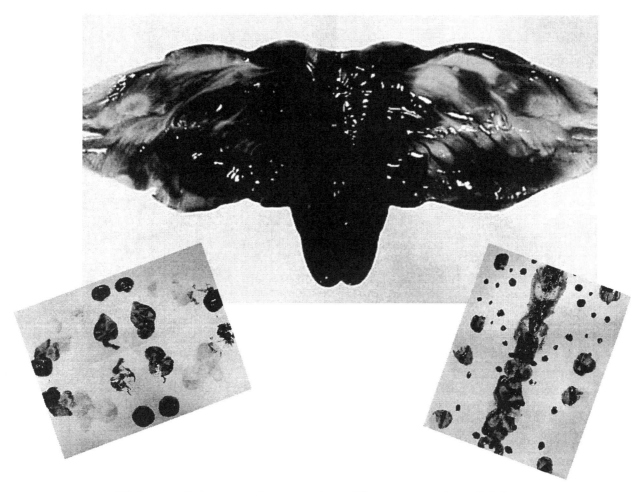

This activity can be used to illustrate the differences between realistic and abstract art.

It can also be used to teach how secondary colors are created from mixing primary colors.

Instructions

1. Fold the paper in half.
2. Open the paper, and on the inside either squirt the tempera paint or blob it on one or both sides of the fold. (Not very much paint is needed to get the desired effect.)
3. Close the folded paper and gently press.
4. Open the paper and let the paint dry.
5. Cut around the created abstraction or mount it on a piece of contrasting construction paper.

Alternate Idea 1

1. Coat a length of string in paint.
2. Place in a squiggly line on one side of a paper folded in half.
3. Close the paper and press together.
4. Open and carefully remove the string. Allow to dry.

Alternate Idea 2

1. Follow the directions as given above.
2. After paint has dried, add more paint to create a totally different effect. It could be more paint adding to the abstractness, or the student might see an object in the

pattern and use more paint to outline or otherwise make it more obvious.

Follow-up Activity

1. During the next class time, have students put their abstractions up on the wall.
2. Let students study them to see what they see in each abstraction.

Baby Birds

MATERIALS

1. FEATHERS IN VARIOUS COLORS (CAN BE PURCHASED AT SUPERSTORES OR HOBBY STORES. EACH BAG HAS ENOUGH FEATHERS TO DO THIS PROJECT WITH TWO OR THREE CLASSES, AND COSTS APPROXIMATELY $2.)
2. SCHOOL GLUE
3. YELLOW OR ORANGE CONSTRUCTION PAPER FOR BEAK
4. CONSTRUCTION PAPER TO GLUE FEATHERS ONTO
5. DARK MARKERS

Baby Birds •
•

Instructions

1. Give each student a small piece of yellow or orange construction paper, and 4 or 5 feathers.
2. Have students glue feathers onto the construction paper in a fan shape.
3. While the glue is drying, have the students cut a triangle out of the yellow or orange construction paper to make the beak.
4. Have the students glue the beak onto the feathers, somewhere near the middle.
5. Using the markers, draw eyes on the feathers above the beak.
6. From here, the students can use their imagination. They can draw legs and other birds in the background, or they might draw a nest the baby bird is sitting in, waiting for mom to bring back food.

Alternate Idea

1. Same process as above.
2. Instead of gluing in a fan shape, glue body and tail feather in place.
3. Using a third feather, cut a piece the size of a half-dollar to use as the head.
4. Draw eyes, beak, and legs with a magic marker.
5. Create a nest by loosely gluing dried peat moss below the bird.
6. Make baby birds by cutting off the ends of feathers and drawing eyes with a black marker. Then glue the babies into the nest.
7. Visit this site for more chick crafts:

   http://www.pittstate.edu/edsc/ssls/ fun.html

Bashful Bats

MATERIALS

1. DIGITAL CAMERA
2. COLOR PRINTER
3. BLACK CONSTRUCTION PAPER
4. GLUE STICKS
5. WHITE CRAYON
6. FISHING LINE
7. BLACK BULLETIN-BOARD PAPER FOR BACKGROUND

Bashful Bats

Instructions

1. Use the digital camera to take a picture of each student's face. (Pictures should be approximately the size of a quarter.)
2. Print the pictures and cut the faces out in a circle.
3. Have students place their outstretched hands on black construction paper. Then, have students trace their hands and cut the hand drawings out.
4. Have students turn the paper over onto the other side, place their hand on the paper again and trace with white crayon. This will cause the hand webbing to be visible on both sides.
5. Have students glue the face to the hand cutouts.
6. Using fishing line, hang the bats from the ceiling with the faces visible from below. This will make the bats look as if they are suspended in air.
7. For an even more special effect, line the walls and ceiling with black paper. Altering the lighting, with a black light, can make this bat mobile even more spectacular.

Additional Ideas

1. Study various aspects of bats.
2. Find websites that detail activities for students.
3. Read *Stellaluna* and other bat books.
4. Purchase plastic bats around Halloween to enhance learning units.
5. Create a bat-related vocabulary list and have students learn specific words during the unit.
6. Find a fact-based video about bats.
7. Find a filmstrip of bats and create a small interest area or corner for students where one or two students at a time can watch the filmstrip.
8. Create a "Batty Bat" puzzle with a bat as the background and the relevant words as the puzzle. There are computer programs that make this very easy.

Beta Fish Facts

MATERIALS

1. BETA FISH AND PLANT IN GLASS CONTAINER
2. ENCYCLOPEDIA
3. INTERNET
4. FOR COMPLETE DETAILS ON HOW TO MAKE YOUR BETA FISH BOWL, ACCESS:

    http://www.pittstate.edu/edsc/ssls/fun.html

    AND CLICK ON THE BETA FISH FACTS LINK

Beta Fish Facts .... :

Experiment

1. How does the fish live when there is no food added to the water?
   + *Microorganisms in the water*
2. How else does the plant help the fish survive?
   + *The plant gives off oxygen, which the fish needs to survive*
3. What does the fish produce that helps the plant?
   + *Carbon dioxide*
4. What is this environment called?
   + *Ecosystem*
5. What is the definition of an ecosystem?
   + *An ecosystem is the network of interactions between organisms and their environment. An ecosystem has both living and nonliv ing components.*

Additional Ideas

Using the Beta Fish Facts link at:

http://www.pittstate.edu/edsc/ssls/fun.html

- Create a diagram of this ecosystem for the beta fish.
- Explore other areas of ecosystems including biomes, community, etc.
- Explore other aspects of the beta fish, like anatomy, history, and behavior.

Bird Bungalow

MATERIALS

1. OLD OR EMPTY SEED PACKETS
2. DECORATIVE SEEDS
3. HOT GLUE GUN AND GLUE
4. BARK
5. A SMALL BIRD IS OPTIONAL—MAY BE PURCHASED AT A CRAFT STORE OR MADE BY STUDENTS
6. FISHING LINE AND PAPER CLIPS—OPTIONAL

Bird Bungalow

Directions/Activity

1. Cut out a small circle in one of the seed packets for the door opening. Use decorative seeds to accent.
2. With adult supervision/help, glue old seed packets together in the shape of a simple house.
3. If the birdhouse is to hang, cut an appropriate length of fishing line and tie a paper clip to either end. When gluing the peak of the roof, be sure to catch the fishing line in the middle, creating a way to hang it.
4. Create a "front porch" by gluing the bark onto the portion of the seed packet that juts out from the bottom.

Use the Bird Bungalow link at:

http://www.pittstate.edu/edsc/ssls/fun.html

for bird coloring pages and ideas such as creating easy bird feeders.

Blowing Bubbles

THIS ACTIVITY HAS SEVERAL OPTIONS. PLEASE READ FIRST TO DECIDE HOW TO BEGIN.

MATERIALS

1. DISH DETERGENT
2. WATER
3. GLYCERIN
4. TEMPERA PAINTS
5. WANDS (SEE BELOW)
6. CONTAINERS FOR BUBBLE SOLUTION (WILL VARY ACCORDING TO AMOUNT PREPARED. FOR VERY LARGE GROUPS, A SMALL PLASTIC SWIMMING POOL OR TUB WILL WORK.)

WANDS:

ANY OBJECT THAT HAS AN OPENING AND CAN BE DIPPED AND HELD CAN BE USED FOR A WAND. SOME IDEAS ARE:

- PLASTIC WRAPS THAT COME ON SIX-PACKS OF SODA MAKE MULTIPLE BUBBLE WANDS.
- USE A 12-INCH PIECE OF COAT HANGER WITH A 10-INCH PIECE OF STRING TIED IN A LOOP ON ONE END.
- CUT THE CENTER OUT OF A PLASTIC LID (YOGURT OR MARGARINE CONTAINER) AND THUMBTACK IT TO A WOODEN CHOPSTICK.
- USE STRAWS, FUNNELS, WHISKS, SMALL COOKIE CUTTERS, ETC., TO MAKE BUBBLES AND MORE BUBBLES.

Blowing Bubbles ·

Magic Bubbles

1 cup liquid tempera paints
2 tbsp. dish detergent
9 oz. water
Wands

Color Bubbles

1 tbsp. glycerin
2 tbsp. dish detergent
9 oz. water
Wands

For large classes or larger wands, double, triple (etc.) the mixture. Then store in appropriate size container so that students can dip wands and create bubbles.

Mixing the Day before the Project Begins

- Mix bubble solution the day before for best results.

- Glycerin is inexpensive and can be purchased in most drugstores. Glycerin makes the bubbles so much better that it's worth the small investment.

Color bubbles can be messy. Be sure to use washable paint like tempera. You can add a little water if the mix is too thick.

Additional Ideas

Allow students to experiment with bubbles and wands that you created one day, and then have them bring their wands from home and use them the next available school day.

For additional bubble activities, click on the Blowing Bubbles link at:

http://www.pittstate.edu/edsc/ssls/fun.html

Buckin' Broncos

MATERIALS

1. A SADDLE (WHICH DOESN'T HAVE TO BE IN GOOD SHAPE)
2. A LARGE PLASTIC BARREL
3. A WOODEN BOX MADE FROM 4 BOARDS
4. A BLANKET WITH A MEXICAN OR NATIVE AMERICAN PATTERN (WHICH CAN BE VERY WORN)
5. PLASTIC SNAKES, ARMADILLOS, ETC., TO ENHANCE THE SETTING

Buckin' Broncos •

Building the Horse

1. Place the blanket on the floor.
2. Clean the saddle.
3. Mount it onto the plastic barrel.
4. Ask a parent, school personnel, or other volunteer to build a wooden box that will hold the barrel snugly.
5. Call the kids in to ride the Buckin' Bronco!

Donations for the Horse

1. Through school newsletters, various agencies, newspapers, etc., ask for a used saddle, which doesn't have to be very good. Also ask for a blanket with a Mexican or Native American pattern to be donated. It doesn't need to be in perfect condition.
2. Find a plastic barrel in a local industry that can be donated. Insure that it stored harmless ingredients.
3. Go to the lumber store and ask for a donation of the necessary wood.

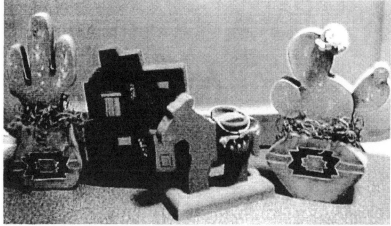

Additional Ideas

Create a Southwest environment by bringing in a cactus, old tin dishware, sunflowers, leather pieces, etc. Kids will especially love some type of plastic snakes to enhance the scene.

Can-Do Castle

MATERIALS—THIS IS A GROUP PROJECT

1. 1 BOX LID OR STURDY RECTANGLE OF CARDBOARD PER GROUP
2. 1 PAPER PLATE PER GROUP
3. HOT GLUE GUN
4. CONSTRUCTION PAPER
5. 1 TOOTHPICK PER GROUP
6. THIN CORKBOARD
7. RIBBONS
8. TEMPERA PAINTS AND PAINTBRUSHES
9. TAPE
10. PATTERNS FROM BACK OF BOOK—PAGES 95-98

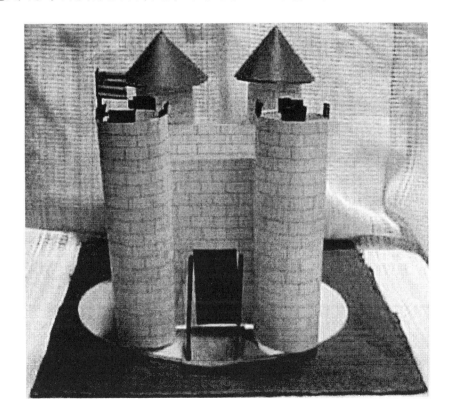

Creating the Castle

1. Paint a 12" x 12" piece of cardboard green for grass.
2. Glue a paper plate upside down on the card board and paint the bottom blue for water.
3. Make four copies of the Tower Pattern on page 96, four copies of the Wall Pattern on page 97, and one copy of the Roof Pattern on page 98 *for each castle.*
4. Let students color the "bricks" of the castle walls and towers to create a more realistic or desirable effect.
5. Cut out a door from construction paper, approximately 1" x 3" and glue it to the bottom of one of the walls.
6. Cut out the patterns as directed for the two front towers.
7. Make the tower patterns into cylinders as directed on the pattern.
8. Make the roof patterns into cones as directed.
9. Glue the roofs onto the two back towers.
10. Cut out the wall patterns and create the walls, approximately 5" x 5", being sure to position the wall with the door at the front bottom of the castle.
11. Glue the towers to the four corners, keeping the door at the front.
12. Affix a strip of corkboard in front of the door like a drawbridge and glue it to the paper plate.
13. Glue ribbon or string to the corners of the door and drawbridge like the chains of a drawbridge would be.
14. Make a small construction paper flag, using the toothpick as the flagpole.
15. Affix the flag to one of the front towers.
16. Decorate the castle with trees, dragons, dolls, etc.

Additional Ideas

For additional ideas and information about castles and heraldry, click on the Can-Do Castle link at:

http://www.pittstate.edu/edsc/ssls/fun.html

Cardboard Cities

MATERIALS

1. A VARIETY OF CARDBOARD BOXES IN DIFFERENT SIZES, BOTH RECTANGULAR AND SQUARE
2. PAINT/MAGIC MARKERS
3. CONSTRUCTION PAPER
4. GLUE STICKS
5. DUCT TAPE
6. CABLE TIES (CAN BE PURCHASED AT ANY HARDWARE STORE OR SUPERCENTER)

Cardboard Cities • • • • • • • • • • • • • • • • • •

Making the City

1. Have the children discuss the buildings in their city or town and identify the buildings that are located there.
2. The anticipated answers will be a grocery store, church, Wal-Mart, school, etc.
3. Then assign each child (or group of children) a building.
4. Have students decorate their buildings.
5. Actually build a city or town from these box buildings.
6. Stack boxes together to create skyscrapers. To secure the boxes together, punch a hole large enough for the cable to go through. Insert a cable tie and tighten.

Additional Ideas

1. Decorate the city/town for festive times like Fall Festival, Christmas, Halloween, etc.
2. Create a committee of children to serve on the "chamber of commerce" and plan a special event, including music, entertainment, etc.
3. Factor in costs and how these costs can be met. (A visit from a real chamber of commerce official can really be helpful.)
4. Click on the Cardboard Cities link at:
   http://www.pittstate.edu/edsc/ssls/fun.html

Speaker Ideas

Inviting these people as speakers to address various topics:
- A firefighter or police officer
- The mayor or a city/town representative
- A person who works at Wal-Mart (perhaps the greeter at the door)
- A representative from the chamber of commerce to speak about the city/town and access the city/town website
- An animal control officer

Castaway Characters

MATERIALS

HAVE EACH STUDENT BRING A DISCARDED ITEM FROM HOME, LIKE:

- OLD TENNIS SHOE
- OLD SHIRT WITH POCKET
- DUCT TAPE
- BALL OF STRING
- STYROFOAM PLATE
- SMALL STYROFOAM CHEST COOLER

Castaway
Characters ·······················

Castaway Preparation

- Do not tell students why they are bringing the items from the previous page.
- Before the activity actually begins, randomly toss equal numbers of items into the two boxes.
- Label the boxes A and B.
- Divide the class into two groups.
- Toss a coin to decide which box goes to which team.

Castaway Activity

1. Have students pretend that they have become castaways on a small island.
2. Allow them to set up the conditions of the island. Ex: location, temperature, fruits, vegetables, etc.
3. For an island to simulate, click on the Castaway Characters link at:
   http://www.pittstate.edu/edsc/ssls/fun.html
4. Hand them the items listed on the previous page.
5. Have students use these items and the conditions of the island and show how they combined both to survive.
6. Have students write a journal of their days on the island.

Additional Ideas

1. Simulate the survivor shows on TV by having students be on a deserted island, but add variables such as rules, dropping of special boxes with special materials and instructions, etc.
2. Assign one-third of the class to be the survivors. Divide the survivors into two groups, where they are competing with one another for survival. Assign one-third to be the team, which creates and drops the special boxes with materials and with rules for the survivors, and the final one-third to be the judges of which survival team best uses the materials.
3. Encourage students to create other possibilities within this scenario.

CD Designs

MATERIALS

1. DISCARDED/BLANK CDs (THESE CAN OFTEN BE DONATED FROM TECH FACILITATORS, PARENTS, AOL FREE CDs, ETC.)
2. CLIP ART/WORD ART/STICKERS/OTHER DECORATIVE ITEMS THAT CAN BE AFFIXED TO CDs
3. MAGNETS
4. CORKBOARD—OPTIONAL
5. DIGITAL CAMERA AND COLOR PRINTER

The possibilities for quick and easy gift-giving are endless!

CD Designs

Directions/Activity

1. Take digital pictures of each student and print them so that they are approximately 1-2 inches square (to cover the hole in the CD). Make the pictures into circles the size of the CD hole.
2. Let students find and use word art, clip art, stickers, cutouts from magazines, and small toys to describe themselves.
3. If possible, laminate the photos and the cutout artwork the students find.
4. Glue the items to the CD, using hot glue.
5. Affix a magnet to the back of each CD.

Optional Idea

Instead of putting a picture of the child's face in the center of the CD, cut a circle of thin corkboard, hot glue it over the center hole of the CD, and add a magnet to the back. Finish the CD as directed, and now you have a magnetic memo holder!

Additional Idea

Explore the properties of light reflection and refraction using the natural prisms in CDs.

Computer Competition

MATERIALS

1. AN OLD COMPUTER THAT HAS BEEN DISCARDED AND DISMANTLED BY THE TECH FACILITATOR
2. CONSTRUCTION PAPER
3. OLD CDs
4. OLD 3.5" FLOPPY DISCS
5. DIGITAL CAMERA

A monster truck from computer parts and old CDs

An oil rig from computer parts

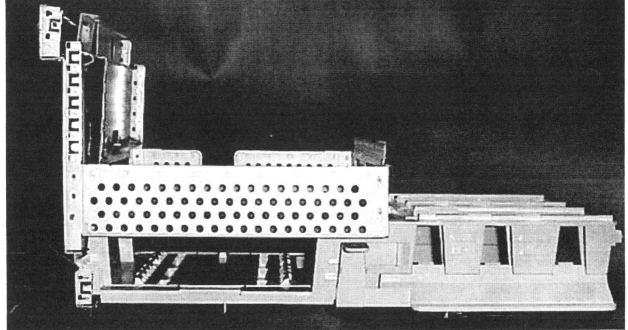

Activity

1. Schedule a time for three or four classes (same or close grade levels) and your technology facilitator to come to the media center together.

2. Ask the tech facilitator to dismantle the computer as the students watch. S/he can remove any sharp or undesirable pieces.

3. After the initial dismantling process, arrange times for each class to come in separately.

4. When the first class comes in, tell the students that they have to make as many items as possible, using the computer parts, old CDs, various plastic lids, and construction paper. Glue and scissors are cheating!

5. Take a digital photo of each creation right away, so parts can be used multiple times.

6. Before the next class comes in, be sure to shuffle all the parts so that the students create their own items.

7. Create a display showing each class and its specific creations, and invite the school to vote for the winner!

Steve, our tech facilitator, dismantles the computer.

A big rig truck from computer and keyboard parts, film can lids, and floppy discs.

Counting Coins

THESE COIN CONTAINERS CAN BE USED IN MATH ACTIVITIES SUCH AS COUNTING AND SORTING. THEY CAN ALSO BE USED TO HOLD PLAY COINS TO USE IN ADDITION AND SUBTRACTION EXERCISES.

Counting Coins •

Making the Counters

1. Obtain used film canisters from any superstore or discount store that has a photo developing center. They will usually give you as many as you want free of charge.
2. Copy the coins below (they will look fine in black and white) and cut them out. Tape them to a canister.
3. Or, let the students cut them out and tape them on.

Additional Ideas

1. You can create the counters with specific numbers like 5, 10, 15, 20, etc. Put the specific number of corn kernels or other similar small items in the canisters for students to count.
2. Use the canisters for multiplication. Create multiple counters of 5, 10, 15, 20, etc. Then have the students picture 2 containers of 5 and let them count how many pieces are inside. This process will allow students to see 2 x 5 = 10.

Dueling Dragon: Paper

MATERIALS

1. PAPER PLATES
2. CONSTRUCTION PAPER
3. WOODEN DOWELS OR CRAFT STICK
4. GLUE
5. CRAYONS OR MARKERS
6. DRAGON FACE PATTERN FROM PAGE 101
7. OPTIONAL—STICK-ON GOOGLY EYES (CAN BE PURCHASED AT DOLLAR STORES, HOBBY STORES, OR SUPERSTORES)

Dueling Dragons • • • • • • • • • • • • • • • • •

Making the Paper Dragon

1. Have students cut horizontal strips of construction paper, approximately 1" wide, and fold them accordion style.
2. Glue these paper strips around the outside of a paper plate.
3. Glue a second paper plate on top of the one with paper strips, with the wooden dowel/stick between them to use as a handle. (Hot glue for the stick works best.)
4. Freehand a flair pattern onto construction paper, and glue it onto the plate.
5. Cut out the Dragon Face Pattern and decorate with glitter, crayons, markers, etc., and glue it onto the center of the flair. If you want, use the googly eyes here.

Dueling Dragons: Fabric

MATERIALS

1. 2 PIECES OF MATERIAL APPROXIMATELY 8" X 11"
2. A STRIP OF FABRIC APPROXIMATELY 4" WIDE AND 4-6' LONG
3. 6-8 PIPE CLEANERS IN VARIOUS COLORS
4. TEMPERA PAINT AND BRUSHES
5. PIECE OF 8" X 11" CARDBOARD
6. PATTERN FROM PAGE 100
7. SEVERAL STRIPS OF RIBBON IN VARIOUS COLORS

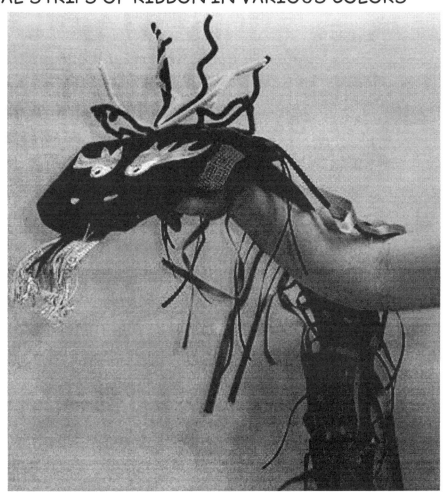

Dueling Dragons

Making the Fabric Dragon

1. Trace the Dragon Face Pattern onto the cardboard and cut it out.
2. Cover the cardboard on both sides with the two 8" x 11" pieces of fabric, using hot glue.
3. Once the fabric is attached, gently bend the head in half along the dotted line.
4. Paint the long strip material as the dragon's body, using lots of colors and abstract designs. Let dry, and then paint the opposite side the same way.
5. While the body is drying, paint a face by tracing the pattern, or simply use it as a guide to create your own.
6. Bend the pipe cleaners in half, attach them in the middle using a paper clip, and then hot glue the paper clip to the dragon's head.
7. Using scrap pieces of fabric, fashion a tongue and beard; then, attach a fabric handle to the underside of the dragon's head.
8. Glue the body to the back of the head, covering the paper clip.
9. Glue small strips of ribbon all the way down the sides of the body.

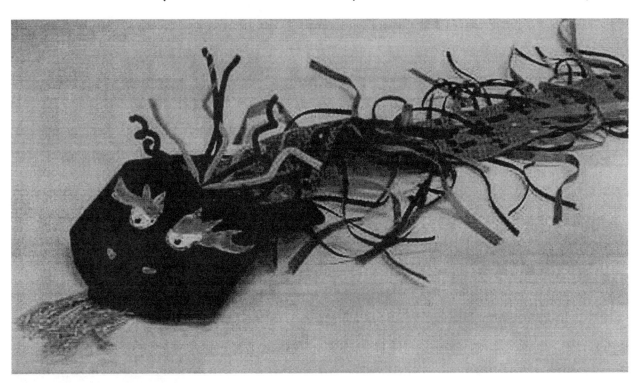

Enormous Eyes

MATERIALS

1. 2 CORDLESS AREA LIGHTS (OFTEN CALLED TOUCH 'N LIGHT OR TAP LIGHTS AND CAN BE FOUND AT SUPERSTORES, HARDWARE STORES, OR FOR THE LOWEST PRICE, DOLLAR STORES)
2. PLENTY OF BATTERIES TO KEEP LIGHTS ON AS LONG AS NEEDED
3. CARDBOARD BOXES
4. SPRAY PAINT
5. SCISSORS
6. DUCT TAPE

Enormous Eyes

Making Cars

1. Spray paint a large box.
2. Cut holes in the front of the box, and secure the lights in the position of headlights. (The teacher may want to cut the holes out ahead of time, using a box knife.)
3. Have students finish the car by cutting out doors and windows. Then they can put on all the detailing and other finishing touches with markers.
4. Alternately, use only one headlight to create a train engine, and add a series of boxes as the railroad cars.

Cardboard Monsters

1. Use the instructions for the cars, but decorate the box as a monster instead.
2. One light can be used to create a cyclops, or use both to create a variety of two-eyed monsters.
3. Also, don't neglect the friendly monsters, which are dominant in children's literature.

Reading Retreats

1. Using a box, which is large enough for children to sit in or lie down in comfortably, follow the instructions for making cars.
2. When you secure the lights in the holes, however, make sure they are mounted on the top, facing down like ceiling lights.
3. Add pillows to sit on or lean against, if you desire.
4. Students can now use this as a private reading spot.
5. Build others if needed and space permits.

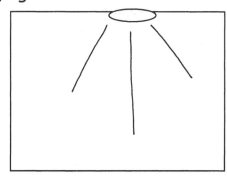

Glass Graphics

MATERIALS

1. A SET OF TEMPERA PAINTS
2. PAINTBRUSH(ES)
3. OPAQUE PROJECTOR
4. IMAGE YOU WISH TO PAINT
5. TAPE
6. WHITE BUTCHER PAPER
7. DARK MARKER
8. A GLASS WINDOW, DOOR, ETC., WHERE YOU WANT TO DISPLAY A GLASS GRAPHIC

Creating the Painting

1. Select an image, and use the opaque projector to increase it to an appropriate size.
2. Trace the image onto the butcher paper. Make sure your lines are bold and easy to see.
3. Take the butcher paper and tape it to the side opposite where you want the image to be, traced side against the glass.
4. Paint the image on the other side of the glass, opposite of the paper. In other words, you should be able to paint using the tracing as a guide, since it is on the other side of the glass.
5. Clean off the painting with soap and water when you no longer want the glass graphic.

Theme Ideas

1. Patriotic themes
2. Seasonal themes
3. Book Fairs
4. Parent/Teacher Conferences
5. Open House welcome
6. Famous people
7. Upcoming events
8. School spirit (mascots, spirit words, etc.)

Happy Sack, Sad Sack

MATERIALS FOR SACKS

1. 3 PAPER OR CLOTH SACKS WITH OR WITHOUT HANDLES
2. 2 PIECES OF BRIGHT YELLOW CONSTRUCTION PAPER
3. 1 BLACK MAGIC MARKER

PREPARING SACKS FOR THE ACTIVITY

1. CUT OUT 2 LARGE CIRCLES FROM THE YELLOW PAPER.
2. DRAW A HAPPY FACE ON ONE SACK, AND A SAD FACE ON THE OTHER.
3. LEAVE THE THIRD SACK PLAIN TO HOLD ITEMS LISTED ON THE OPPOSITE PAGE.

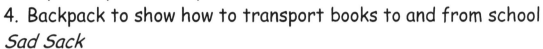

Materials for Inside the Sacks

Happy Sack
1. Bar of soap
2. Bookmark
3. Picture of shelves to show that books should be kept in a protected place
4. Backpack to show how to transport books to and from school

Sad Sack
1. Pictures of a cat and dog, to show that animals can tear up books
2. Scissors to show that pages of books can be cut up by smaller children
3. Tape to show that books can get torn
4. A book that has been written on or in
5. A book that has "dog ears" instead of bookmarks
6. Jars of peanut butter or jelly, to show how sticky fingers ruin books
    Note: all of the materials should be in the third, unmarked sack at the beginning of the activity.

Activity

1. Show the children both the Happy and the Sad sacks, explaining that they represent how books would feel about what is done to them.
2. Show the children the third sack, which contains the items such as the soap, bookmark, or scissors.
3. Lift each item out of the third sack, and ask the children if this item belongs in the Happy Sack or the Sad Sack. Ask them why after each decision is made.

Other Activities

The Happy Sack/Sad Sack activity can be applied to many other themes, such as:

~ Playground behavior ~ Bus behavior ~ Cafeteria behavior ~
~ Classroom behavior ~ Caring ~ Sharing ~

Imaginative Impressionists

MATERIALS
1. PAST CALENDERS THAT FEATURE NATURE SCENES
2. TEMPERA PAINTS AND BRUSHES
3. PAPER
4. WATER AND PAPER FOR BRUSH CLEANUP
5. MASKING TAPE TO SECURE CALENDAR PAGES DURING PAINTING ACTIVITY

Before

After

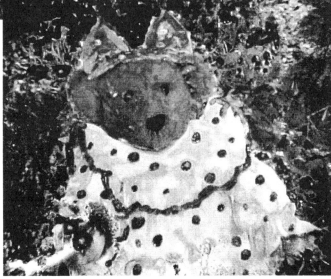

Imaginative
Impressionists
· ·
·

Instructions

1. Separate the pages of the calendar and students to select one each.
2. Give each student a brush, paints, and a small container of water for cleaning the brush.
3. Discuss how the impressionists put very small lumps or dots of paint onto the canvas, creating an *impressionist* painting. Tell how the paintings were best viewed from a distance, rather than up close. Also, discuss that impressionists often used brighter colors than those found in nature. Examples of impressionism can be found by clicking the Imaginative Impressionists link at:
    http://www.pittstate.edu/edsc/ssls/fun.html
5. Tell the students they will simulate this painting style.
6. Have students begin dotting small spots of tempera paint, using the original calendar page as a guide, until the entire picture is finished.
7. When the paintings are finished and completely dry, have students create a display for others to see.

Additional Ideas

Click on the Imaginative Impressionists link at:
    http://www.pittstate.edu/edsc/ssls/fun.html
for more ideas and information about painters and painting.
Examples of some of the pages the site has:
+ Painters   + Painting for kids
+ Painters' birthdays   + How to paint a dolphin
+ History of painting   + Worldwide art museums

Community Connection

Explore your community, looking for blank walls that could use some enhancement. Possibilities include nursing home walls, indoor walking tracks, community center walls, etc. Show the paintings the students have created from the calendar project and ask if students can paint similar pictures on the walls. It's a win-win situation for both the students and the community!

Magical Myths

MATERIALS

1. SCRAPS OF MATERIAL (YOU NEED ENOUGH FOR EACH CHILD TO HAVE AT LEAST ONE PIECE, AND FOR SOME STUDENTS TO HAVE SEVERAL. THESE CAN BE OBTAINED BY SENDING OUT REQUESTS. ALTHOUGH MANY PEOPLE NO LONGER SEW, THEY OFTEN STILL HAVE SCRAPS OF MATERIAL AND WOULD LIKE TO DONATE THEM.)
2. ENOUGH SAFTEY PINS FOR EACH STUDENT
3. SMALL PERFORMANCE AREA
4. AGE APPROPRIATE MYTHS

Magical Myths

Activity

1. Ask students to share their ideas of how the earth began, how humans were created, where the stars came from, etc.
2. Discuss the definition of a myth, and discuss how creation myths (of the earth, of people, of animals, of the sky, etc.) can be found in all cultures and mythologies, from ancient Greek to Native American.
3. Select an age appropriate myth and read it to the students.
4. Talk about the myth and then talk about how wonderful and exciting imaginations are.
5. Ask the students "If you could be anything or anyone in the world, who or what would you be?"
6. After the discussion, let students select 2-3 material scraps.
7. Tell students they can be anything they want to be.
8. Allow and encourage students to wrap the material around themselves to simulate their real or mythical personification.
9. Assist students and encourage them to help each other fasten material.
10. Ask the students to come up on the performance area, one at a time, and tell the audience who they are.

Additional Ideas

1. Use the material to decorate shelves, tables, etc., which will add instant life and color to the room.
2. Have students select material with a pattern, and then have them cut around the pattern.
3. Then, have the students glue this fabric cutout to a piece of construction paper.
4. Use as a teaching moment, or as an inspiration/illustration for a student's creative story.

Mancala Mania

MATERIALS

1. EGG CARTONS
2. THIN CARD STOCK
3. TAPE
4. TEMPERA PAINT AND BRUSHES
5. 48 PLAYING PIECES (SMOOTH GLASS BEADS WORK WELL)

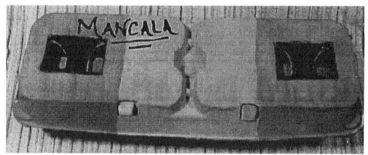

Mancala Mania

Creating the Game

1. Using the tempera paint, decorate the egg cartons.
2. Using the thin card stock and tape, create two shallow boxes that will fit inside the egg carton when closed (see picture).

Playing Mancala
Two Players

Object of the Game:

To be the player who holds the most game pieces in his or her tray at the end of the game.

To play (General Rules):

- Place 4 game pieces in each of the 12 cups, but leave the larger end trays (the mancalas) empty.
- The youngest player takes the first move.
- The first player takes all of the game pieces from one of his/her small bowls (never his mancala) and drops one game piece in each bowl (going counterclockwise) until s/he has no game pieces left.
- Player two does the same.
- If a player comes to his/her own mancala, s/he drops one game piece in it and continues to play as normal.
- If a player comes to his/her opponent's mancala, s/he skips it, and then continues on with normal play.
- When one or both players run out of game pieces, the game is over. Whoever has the most game pieces in his/her mancala wins the game.

For illustrated variations on the general rules, click on the Mancala Mania link at:

http://www.pittstate.edu/edsc/ssls/fun.html

Me, Myself, and I

USE THIS FOR OPEN HOUSE AND/OR OTHER SIMILAR EVENTS. BE SURE TO SEND OUT NOTICES TO PARENTS TO BRING THEIR CAMERAS BECAUSE THIS EVENT WILL NEED TO BE ADDED TO SCRAPBOOKS.

MATERIALS
EACH STUDENT WILL NEED TO BRING THE FOLLOWING FROM HOME:

- 1 PAIR OF JEANS OR BOTTOM OF SWEATS OR SLACKS, ETC.
- 1 LONG-SLEEVED TOP (CAN BE A JERSEY, WHATEVER THE STUDENT WANTS)
- 1 PAIR OF SHOES (USUALLY SNEAKERS)
- 1 HAT (IF DESIRED)

TEACHER WILL PROVIDE
- DIGITAL CAMERA
- SAFETY PINS (SEVERAL PACKAGES)
- 4 PAPER PLATES PER STUDENT (CHEAP ONES WORK WELL)
- CRAYONS
- LOTS OF SCRAP NEWSPAPER OR PAPER, WHICH WILL BE USED FOR STUFFING
- WOODEN STICKS OR PAINT STIRRERS.

Me, Myself, and I

Making Yourself

1. Stuff the shirt and pants with scrap paper or newspaper. Pin together.
2. Use a digital camera to take close-up pictures of the students' faces. (Students can pair up and do this part themselves.)
3. Print the pictures using either a color or black and white printer.
4. Have students cut out their head shot.
5. Tape a wooden stick to the back of the head shot.
6. Stick the head onto the student's stuffed clothes, and position it as needed.
7. Have students trace their hands onto paper plates, color them, and cut them out. (You can also take digital pictures of hands and have students cut them out like the faces.)
8. Stick the paper hands into the ends of the sleeves.
9. If needed, use safety pins to hold hands in place.
10. Place a hat onto the student's second self.
11. Position the student's second self at the desk with props such as books, paper, and pencils.
12. If time is a problem, then just create the head shot on a stick.

Mighty Magnets

MATERIALS

1. SEVERAL MAGNETS, ALL THE SAME SIZE
2. PAPER CLIPS (SEVERAL BOXES)
3. VARIOUS ITEMS BOTH MAGNETIC AND NONMAGNETIC
   (DRINKING STRAWS, RUBBER BANDS, ALUMINUM CANS, ETC.)
4. WORKSHEET FROM PAGE 99
5. PENCILS FOR STUDENTS TO RECORD DATA

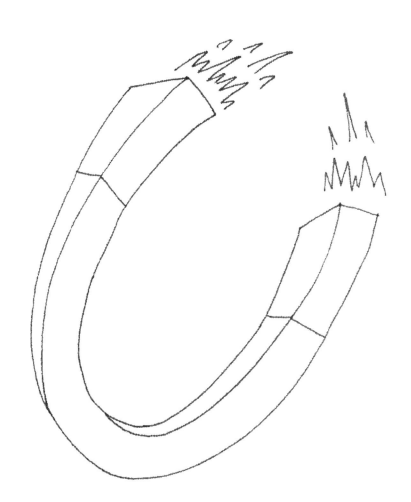

• •

Is It Magnetic?

1. Do not give students the magnets yet.
2. Place all the objects collected (both magnetic and nonmagnetic) in front of the students.
3. Hand out copies of the Magnetic Activity Worksheet on page 99.
4. In the first column, have the students write the items to be tested for magnetism. In other words, is a straw magnetic?
5. In the second column, have the students write their predictions of whether or not the item is magnetic.
6. Now, divide the students into groups and give each group a magnet and one of each of the items to be tested. Let them test their predictions and record the results.

How Strong Is the Magnet?

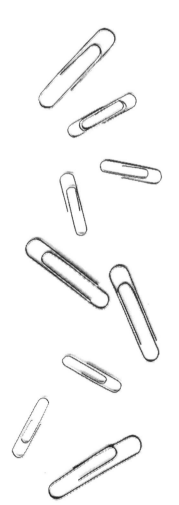

1. Demonstrate the magnetic property of a paper clip.
2. Ask the students to predict how many paper clips one magnet can attract and hold. Use the same handout for responses.
3. With the students still in their groups, hand out an adequate number of paper clips for students to test their predictions.

Related Magnetic Websites

Click on the Mighty Magnets link at:

http://www.pittstate.edu/edsc/ssls/fun.html

for information, fun facts, experiments, and lesson plans dealing specifically with magnets.

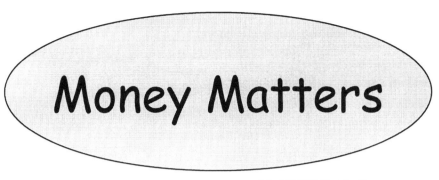

Money Matters

MATERIALS
1. SET OF FAKE MONEY (WAL-MART NOW HAS FAKE CURRENCY THAT LOOKS LIKE THE NEW BILLS)
2. LIBRARY MEDIA CENTER
3. CASH BOX LIKE THE ONES THAT SCHOOLS USE FOR CONCESSION MONEYS, ETC.

Money Matters •••••••••••••••••••••

Business Experiment

1. Have students analyze the library media center and create a small bookstore.
2. Encourage students to create the name, arrangement, and other details of their bookstore.
3. Allow students to select the "owner," "employees," establish hours of operation, etc.
4. Suggest that students look at their business from every possible aspect, such as marketing, by creating flyers, brochures, etc.
5. Distribute a set amount of fake money to the students who will be the "customers."
6. Open the bookstore.
7. Allow students to purchase books with their fake money. (New books have their prices on the book jacket. You may want to set a price for all older books or those that don't have a price anywhere on them.)
8. You can include a tax rate to teach about percentages for higher grade levels.
9. Teach students about appropriate behaviors for people who work in service jobs such as retail and sales.

Additional Ideas

1. Have students create a return policy.
2. Discuss shoplifting and how it impacts the buyer and the seller.
3. Study marketing and how it impacts business.
4. Ask a small business owner to speak to the class, using an open-ended dialogue.
5. Ask a local bookstore owner/operator to come and speak to the class.
6. Ask the library media specialist to discuss how the media center compares/contrasts to a business operation.

Mystery Masks

MATERIALS

1. EMPTY AND CLEAN ONE-GALLON PLASTIC MILK OR WATER JUGS
2. SCISSORS
3. NEWSPAPER CUT INTO STRIPS
4. FLOUR AND WATER PASTE
5. YARN
6. MAGIC MARKERS
7. ORNAMENTAL OBJECTS LIKE FEATHERS, LEATHER STRIPS, SEQUINS, ETC.
8. HOT GLUE GUN
9. TEMPERA PAINTS

Mystery Masks

Making the Masks

Note: You many want to complete steps 1 and 2 prior to the beginning of class.

1. Remove the handle section from the milk container, leaving a large enough plastic piece to use for the mask. (Notice that the jug already looks somewhat like a mask.)
2. Cut three holes on each side of the mask and thread the yarn through each hole. Allow enough yarn to reach the back of the students' heads and be tied into a bow.
3. Using the papier-mâché recipe from page 94, cover the mask so the tempera paint will have a base to which it can adhere.
4. Cut holes to accommodate the eyes and mouth.
5. Paint the dried mask with tempera paints, and add feathers and other decorative items as desired.

Additional Ideas

1. Allow students to create the masks and then write a play that matches them.
2. Alternately, have students write a play and then create masks that match it.
3. Invite middle or high school art students to assist with the mask making.
4. Pair middle or high school students with younger students to create plays.
5. Invite an African American or Native American scholar to discuss masks and the significance of masks in the history and culture of their people.

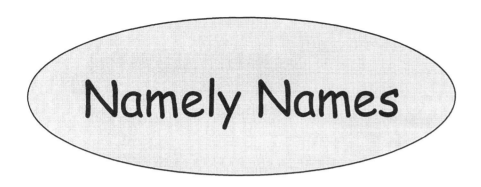

Namely Names

MATERIALS

1. WHITE PAPER FOR STUDENTS TO CREATE THEIR NAME POEM
2. LASER STATIONARY (ENOUGH FOR EACH STUDENT TO HAVE ONE SHEET)
3. COMPUTERS FOT STUDENTS TO USE
4. DIGITAL CAMERA

Namely Names

Creating the Name Poems

1. Instruct students to write their names with the alignment on the left margins.
2. Using each letter of their name as the first letter, have the students write a few words to describe how they see themselves.
3. Have students type their name poems on the computer, encouraging them to experiment with fonts and type sizes, keeping in mind that the poem must fit onto one page.
4. Have the students take digital pictures of each other, and then help them insert their picture onto the page of their poem.
5. When students have finished formatting their poems, have them print their names.

Additional Ideas

1. Students can additionally make a frame (out of cardboard, markers, crayons, glitter, etc.) and present to parents as a gift.
2. Students can create a class bulletin board.
3. Students can create a class journal.
4. Older students can pair up with younger students and help them create similar projects.
5. Each student can place the name poem on his or her desk for open house or parent/teacher conferences.
6. Students can save their poems on the computer and send them through e-mail to a pen pal, grandparent, etc.

Jubilant
Animal lover
New big sister
Everyone's friend

KIND TO OTHERS
YAHTZEE PLAYER
LIKES TO PLAY VIDEO GAMES
EATS PIZZA ALL THE TIME

Nature Notes

MATERIALS
1. CONSTRUCTION PAPER CUT OR FOLDED INTO FOURTHS, LIKE NOTE CARDS
2. FRESH LEAVES FROM A NATURE WALK
3. TEMPERA PAINTS

Nature Notes

Instructions

1. Take students on a nature walk and allow them to collect various types and sizes of fresh leaves.
2. Hand out sheets of construction paper to the students.
3. Have students dip one of their leaves into whatever color of tempera paint they choose, and then press the paint side to the construction paper and then quickly remove it. This will leave a leaf print on the note paper.
4. Let students also gather small flowers, weeds, interesting seeds, etc., and let them incorporate these into their nature note cards.

Additional Ideas

1. For Halloween, use orange construction paper with black tempera paints.
2. For Christmas, use red paper and green paint, or vice versa. Or, use blue and white for Hanukkah.
3. In spring, near Easter, use pastels.
4. For Thanksgiving, use brown paint on yellow or orange paper, and encourage students to try to make turkeys out of leaves that have four or five prominent points.

Click on the Nature Notes link at:

http://www.pittstate.edu/edsc/ssls/fun.html

for information about nature and conservancy both
in the United States and around the world, specific
lesson plans, and other fun stuff.

Once Upon an Ocean

MATERIALS

1. WALL IN THE MEDIA CENTER OR CLASSROOM (THAT CAN BE PAINTED ON)
2. LOCAL ARTIST (COULD BE A WILLING PARENT OR STUDENT)
3. PAINTS AND BRUSHES
4. SEA SHELLS
5. SEA ANIMALS THAT STUDENTS CAN HOLD
6. BOOKS RELATED TO OCEAN CREATURES
7. PLASTIC SHARKS AND OTHER SEA CREATURES
8. FISHING NET LIKE THOSE USED NEAR OR IN AN OCEAN
9. SAND BUCKET AND TROWEL

Once Upon an Ocean ....

Creating the Ocean

1. Ask an artist (talented student or parent) to paint an ocean scene where you get the effect of the wall being made of glass, letting people peer into the lower depths of the sea.
2. Decorate the wall with the net.
3. Add shells, sharks, bucket, etc.
4. Add books that relate to the ocean.
5. Add any other manipulative items that pertain to the ocean scene: plastic starfish, lobsters, sea snakes, etc.

Additional Ideas

1. Send out a request to school personnel and parents for any ocean related items. Items such as blowfish, sand dollars, sea stars, etc., are ideal.
2. To use smaller, more fragile items in the display, place them in clear plastic containers, and pad them with tissue on one side. This way, students can see them up close and hold them, but the items won't break.
3. Send out a request for the donation (or loan) of a ship in a bottle, or other interesting, hard-to-find items.
4. Use an aquarium in conjunction to study fish behavior.

5. If there is a large, public aquarium in your community, take a field trip, or ask the aquarium to send a speaker to your class.

Party Piñata

MATERIALS

1. PAPIER-MÂCHÉ RECIPE
2. TEMPERA PAINTS AND BRUSHES
3. TISSUE OR CREPE PAPER
4. VARIOUS OTHER DECORATIVE ITEMS

Party Piñata •

Directions/Activity

1. Cover a large balloon with the papier-mâché, and let dry overnight.
2. Cover the newspaper strips with the tissue/crepe paper. Use tempera paint as your glue. This will keep the newspaper print from bleeding through.
3. Cut tissue paper into pieces approximately 2" square.
4. When the paint has finished drying, cover the body of the piñata with the tissue paper squares, using the pomping technique (See page 94).
5. Cut a hole about 1"-2" in diameter on the top of the piñata to fill with candy.

C	I	N	C	O
1	20	24	33	48
7	13	25	37	46
4	17	FREE	35	42
3	12	29	36	47
10	14	22	31	49

Additional Ideas

As an activity to be used in conjuction with Cinco de Mayo, make a Cinco game. Take a Bingo game, and on each playing card replace the "B" and "G" with "C." When calling the numbers, say "C" when "B" or "G" come up. It will not lead to too much confusion because the numbers are still associated with the specific columns. In other words C3 will be in the first column and C36 will be in the third. If a player "Cinco's," but calls out "Bingo," the win doesn't count, and the caller continues until a new winner "Cinco's."

For additional information and ideas, click on the Party Piñata link at:
http://www.pittstate.edu/edsc/ssls/fun.html

Performing Puppets

MATERIALS

1. USED SOCKS FOR PUPPETS
2. FELT, BUTTONS, ANY KIND OF BEADS, OR ANY OTHER OLD KNICK KNACKS FOR MAKING THE EARS, EYES, ETC.
3. GLUE
4. SCISSORS
5. MAGIC MARKERS
6. LARGE, SIDE-BY-SIDE REFRIGERATOR BOX
7. SQUARE PIECE OF PLYWOOD THAT IS LARGER THAN THE BOTTOM OF THE BOX BY SIX SQUARE INCHES.
8. LARGE MATERIAL SCRAPS

Puppet by Gina, age 10, who also wears glasses.

Performing Puppets

Making the Puppets

1. Give each student a sock.
2. Show examples of puppets purchased from a store.
3. Tell students to use their imagination and create their own puppets. Let them use anything available to them to create the puppet—buttons for eyes, felt for ears, old single earrings for a nose, etc.

Building a Puppet Theater

1. Get a large box from a side-by-side refrigerator.
2. Cut out the back of the box so that you have two sides, the front, the top, and the bottom.
3. Attach the plywood to the bottom of the box, creating a stable platform that will not tip or fall.
4. Cut a rectangular window from the front of the box to create a stage.
5. Use material scraps and sturdy wire to create curtains. Secure the wire across the top of the window. Then, hang the material over the wire with most of the material hanging down and facing out. Staple the two layers to create a pocket that the wire is already running through.
6. Cover the outside of the puppet theater with wallpaper that looks magical. Or, let students decorate the outside themselves, using tempera paint.

Creating Plays

1. Students can write plays and perform them using their puppets and theater.
2. Videotape the students in their rehearsal stages and let them view their performance for self-critiquing.
3. Videotape the final performance and allow the students to view in celebration of their creativity.

Alternate Ideas

1. Instead of building a theater, push two desks together and drape large material scraps, rugs, blankets, etc., over them to hide the open space between the legs. Students can sit behind the fabric and use the desk as the puppet stage.
2. Ask teachers to let your students perform their plays for other classes. In this case, students might want to perform plays of well-known stories or fables, in addition to their own creations.

Personal Palette

MATERIALS

1. FILM CAN
2. BUTTER TUB OR COFFEE CAN LID
3. HOT GLUE

Making the Palette

1. Obtain used film canisters from any superstore or discount store that has a photo developing center. They will usually give you as many as you want free of charge.
2. Glue a canister to the bottom (edges up) of a plastic lid from a coffee can, butter tub, etc., with hot glue.
3. Keep the canister lid, making the palette easy to use class after class.
4. You can also put the lid back on the water part of the palette, then students can carry their own palette without making a mess.
5. The individual paints will eliminate potential contamination problems from child to child.

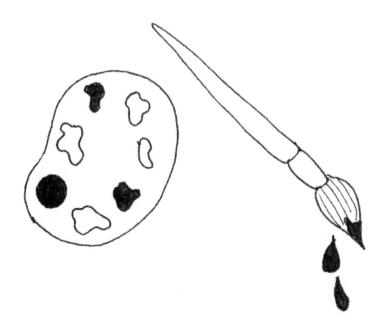

Puppies for a Price

MATERIALS

1. OLD NEWSPAPERS (AT LEAST ONE PER STUDENT)
2. THE FOLLOWING SALE ADS CAN BE PASTED INTO A REAL NEWSPAPER PAGE.
3. ENCYCLOPEDIAS (PRINT OR ELECTRONIC)

Puppies for a Price

Activity

1. Give students a newspaper and tell them to find the classified page where you have taped the "puppy ad."
2. When they find the page, tell them to find the puppy in their ad in the encyclopedia/Internet and report back to the class what the advertisement actually tells about the puppy.

Additional Activities

1. Younger children can learn the song, "How Much Is That Doggy in the Window?"
2. Children can bring pictures of their pets and create a bulletin board.
3. Invite a vet or zookeeper to talk about animals.
4. Invite a dog groomer to talk about grooming animals.
5. Assist children in a small fund-raiser, to raise money for the local animal shelter.

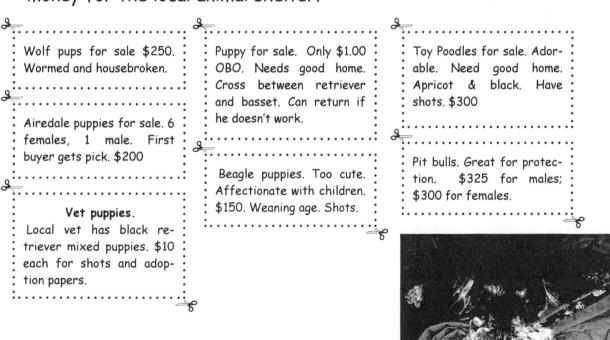

Wolf pups for sale $250. Wormed and housebroken.

Airedale puppies for sale. 6 females, 1 male. First buyer gets pick. $200

Vet puppies.
Local vet has black retriever mixed puppies. $10 each for shots and adoption papers.

Puppy for sale. Only $1.00 OBO. Needs good home. Cross between retriever and basset. Can return if he doesn't work.

Beagle puppies. Too cute. Affectionate with children. $150. Weaning age. Shots.

Toy Poodles for sale. Adorable. Need good home. Apricot & black. Have shots. $300

Pit bulls. Great for protection. $325 for males; $300 for females.

Rescued Refuse

MATERIALS

1. CONSTRUCTION PAPER
2. ODDS AND ENDS FROM AROUND THE SCHOOL THAT NORMALLY GET DISCARDED (BOXES, JUGS, STRING, OLD CDs, PACKING MATERIALS—BUBBLE WRAP AND PEANUTS, ETC.)
3. HOT GLUE AND GLUE GUN
4. TACKY GLUE
5. SCISSORS
6. RINSED-OUT PLASTIC POP BOTTLES

Meet Rescued Refuse Ralph

Created from an old pop bottle, scrap construction paper, and sugar dyed with food coloring.

Precontest

1. First, decide how many groups you want to compete.
2. Then, equally divide the junk into one box per group.
3. Be sure to have at least one glue gun, several pairs of scissors, and other supplies for each group.
4. The teacher should keep the contents of the junk boxes hidden until the contest begins.
5. The teacher should determine the length of time that will be allowed the teams during the competition.

Rules

1. Each group gets one box of junk and necessary supplies.
2. Each group has to use every piece of junk in the box.
3. Group cooperation and leadership will be considered by the judges (or teacher) in determining the winner.
4. Each group must build something that would be used in a school, either real or imaginary.
5. At the next class meeting (or for another class), each group will present its project and "sell" it.
6. After the final presentations, the class or audience or selected judges will vote for a winner. The teacher will take into account the results of the popular vote and the cooperation and leadership that was (or was not) demonstrated during the project building to determine the overall winners.

Let the Games Begin!

Regal Rocks

MATERIALS

1. A ROCK FOR EACH STUDENT
2. DIGITAL CAMERA
3. INTERNET ACCESS

Rose Rock

Turquoise

Calcite

Barite

Wavellite

Regal Rocks

Internet Identity

1. Give each student a rock.
2. Have students take a digital picture of the rock.
3. Ask your technology facilitator for assistance in posting students' digital pictures on the Internet, so that students can ask for help in identifying their specific rock from rock enthusiasts in cyber-space.
4. Have students discuss the responses they get as they come in.

Additional Ideas

1. Almost every area has a local rock hound or two. Ask if one would be interested in assisting with this project.
2. Local mining/mineral organizations are often willing to help.
3. Contact state and national organizations for assistance and materials.
4. Have students bring rocks from home.
5. Remember that the Internet and e-mail can connect your class with people who are willing to help.
6. Find small rocks, and using markers or paint, let students give them a face. It's their own pet rock!
7. For cool information about rocks and a great example on one school's rock collection, click on the Regal Rocks link at:

http://www.pittstate.edu/edsc/ssls/fun.html

Scarecrow Season

MATERIALS

1. FRAME (FAKE CHRISTMAS TREE STAND AND TRUNK STRUCTURE IS PERFECT)
2. DISCARDED PAIR OF OVERALLS, COVERALLS, OR JUMPSUIT
3. OLD FLANNEL SHIRT
4. STRAW HAT
5. YELLOW PAPER CUT INTO STRIPS FOR "STRAW"
6. MAGIC MARKERS
7. CONSTRUCTION PAPER
8. SCISSORS
9. TAPE AND DUCT TAPE
10. POWER STAPLER
11. CLEAN PAPER TRASH

Use this concept to create a school mascot or Outstanding Player of the Week. The player's uniform can be borrowed and a digital picture can make the representation fun.

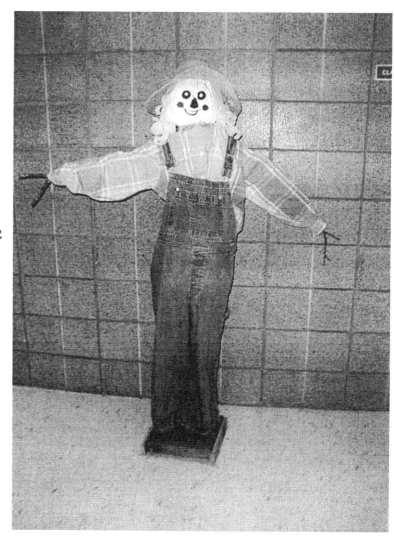

Making the Scarecrow

1. Use the frame structure.
2. Slide an old pair of overalls onto the frame.
3. Loosely tape (duct tape works best) the bottoms of the overalls to the frame.
4. Fill the bottom of the overalls with clean trash.
5. Tuck a flannel shirt inside the top of the overalls and loosely attach the sleeves to the frame.
6. Stuff with clean trash until the desired effect is achieved.
7. Tape the collar of the shirt to the frame.
8. Create a face by stuffing the "straw" into the neck hole of the shirt and arranging the ends that stick out into a face shape. Or, use a paper plate and draw facial features.
9. Make eyes, nose, etc., out of the colored construction paper.
10. Add a straw hat to the top of the scarecrow.
11. Surround with additional props such as plants, flowers, a crow, etc.

Snowmen & Stuff

MATERIALS

1. PIECE OF WOOD, APPROXIMATELY 2" X 4'
2. HEAVY BLOCK OF WOOD, APPROXIMATELY 12" X 12" (A FAKE CHRISTMAS TREE STAND CAN BE USED INSTEAD)
3. THREE WHITE TRASH BAGS
4. MAGIC MARKERS
5. STICKS FOR ARMS AND GLOVES FOR HANDS
6. POWER STAPLER
7. CLEAN PAPER TRASH
8. STOCKING HAT OR OTHER HAT OF CHOICE AND SCARF

Making the Snowman

1. Attach the 2" x 4' wood strip to the heavy square block or use fake Christmas tree stand.
2. Make a small puncture hole in the bottom of one trash bag and slide it down the post of the stand.
3. The opening of the sack should be completely accessible. Fill it full of clean paper trash, until the sack fills out and looks like the bottom roll of a snowman. (White balloons can be used. Partially inflated are best.)
4. Pull the top together and connect to the post.
5. Repeat the process for the second roll of the snowman, but fill the bag with less trash or fewer balloons to reduce the size.
6. Repeat the process once more for the head, filling it with even less.
7. On construction paper, use magic markers to color two eyes, a carrot nose, and a mouth.
8. Cut out buttons.
9. Or, take a digital picture of a student or teacher

Additional Ideas

1. Create a snowperson family.
2. Place white sheets on the floor, under the snowmen, to simulate snow on the ground.
3. Bring in props such as books, toys, etc., to create themes.
4. Click on the Snowmen & Stuff link at:
   http://www.pittstate.edu/edsc/ssls/fun.html

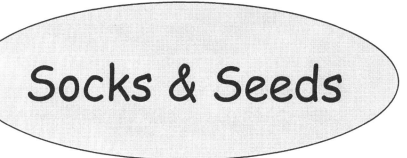

Socks & Seeds

MATERIALS

1. ONE CLEAN, WORN, ADULT SOCK PER STUDENT
2. ONE MAGNIFYING GLASS FOR EVERY STUDENT OR PAIR OF STUDENTS
3. WHITE POSTER BOARD THAT CAN BE CUT INTO 3" X 3" SQUARES
4. PENS OR PENCILS

Seed Experiment

1. Take students outside.
2. Give each student a sock.
3. Instruct students to slide the sock over one shoe.
4. Allow students to walk around in grass for a designated period of time, perhaps at recess.
5. Have students carefully remove the sock.
6. Take students inside and have each examine the sock under a magnifying glass.
7. Let students discover the native seeds, etc.
8. Instruct students to take the seed from the sock and glue the seed to a small white poster board square for labeling.
9. Use various resources (either books or Internet) to label each seed.

Alternate Idea

If any of the seeds are plants that flower, or grow easily, Consider starting a small classroom garden. Or, this could be a good beginning for a unit about plants.

Tablecloths as Tools

MATERIALS

1. PLASTIC TABLECLOTH (CAN BE PURCHASED AT DOLLAR STORES, BUT BE SURE TO BUY THE TABLECLOTHS THAT HAVE FLANNEL BACKS. PLAIN PLASTIC CLOTHS WILL NOT WORK.)
2. MAGIC MARKERS
3. OPAQUE PROJECTOR
4. OBJECT(S) TO BE TRACED

An example of how a math flashlight activity might look.

1	2	3	4
5	6	7	8
9	10	11	12
13	14	15	16
17	18	19	20

Making Tablecloth Banners

1. You can adjust the tablecloth to be any size banner that you want by cutting it to that size

2. Have students use opaque projector to enlarge image to be copied. Students can use a variety of colors to enhance image.

3. Students can then write words on banner.

4. Banner can be doubled at top for durability and attached in a variety of ways. (Will be much stronger than paper banners.)

Flashlight Activity

This can be used for a variety of educational activities. We'll use math as an example. Sight words or colors are other possibilities.

1. First, write the numbers 1-20, in numerical order (4-5 to a row) on the cloth.

2. Then, give each child a customized addition, subtraction, multiplication, and division worksheet.

3. To check a student's work, instead of looking at the written problem, ask the student what his/her answer was for a specific problem. Using a flashlight, the student will point to the number that is his/her answer.

4. While the teacher is working one at a time with each student turn by turn, the other students can continue their own work.

5. Alternately, the teacher can pose problems to the class and instruct all the students to point to the correct answer with the flashlight. While the weaker students will follow the stronger ones, the correct answers will still be reinforced.

Additional Banner Ideas/Occasions

~Spirit Day~   ~Congratulatory~   ~Teacher of the Year~
~Good-Bye Banners for students or staff~   ~Open House~
~Upcoming Events~
~Parent/Teacher Conference~

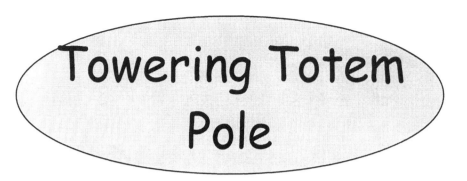

Towering Totem Pole

MATERIALS

1. FILM CANISTERS (CAN BE OBTAINED FROM ANY SUPERSTORE OR DISCOUNT STORE THAT HAS A PHOTO DEVELOPING CENTER)
2. CONSTRUCTION PAPER
3. MAGIC MARKERS
4. TAPE

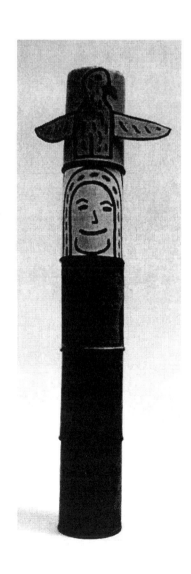

Making the Totem Pole

1. Using markers and construction paper, let students draw totem levels that will fit around discarded film canisters.
2. Using tape, have the students wrap the art around the canister.
3. Carefully insert the top of one canister into the opening of another. They should stay without any adhesive or tape. Repeat until the totem pole is assembled.
4. Encourage students to be creative—for example, 3-D wings on a bird.

Additional Idea

Make musical shakers with the totem poles or individual film canisters. Fill the canister with dry corn, beans, or rice and seal tightly. Experiment with the sounds different grains create.

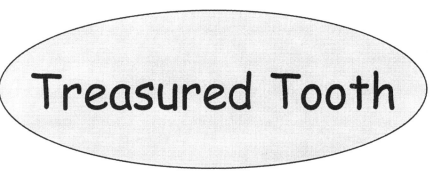

Treasured Tooth

MATERIALS

1. FILM CANISTERS
2. TAPE
3. COPIED TEETH

Making the Tooth Holders

1. Obtain used film canisters from any superstore or discount store that has a photo developing center. They will usually give you as many as you want free of charge.

2. Copy the teeth below (they will look fine in black and white) and cut them out. Draw a happy face with a black fine-tip marker. Glue them to a canister using a glue stick or rubber cement.

3. Or, let the student who has lost a tooth cut it out and decorate it as she or he wishes, then glue it on.

Additional Ideas

For information about teeth and oral hygiene as well as games and lots of activities, click on the Treasured Tooth link at:

http://www.pittstate.edu/edsc/ssls/fun.html

Veggie Vignettes

VARIOUS VEGETABLES, FROM CELERY TO GREEN PEPPERS, ARE
USED TO CREATE THESE FLORAL DESIGNS!
1. VARIOUS FRUITS AND VEGETABLES
2. TEMPERA PAINTS
3. PAPER

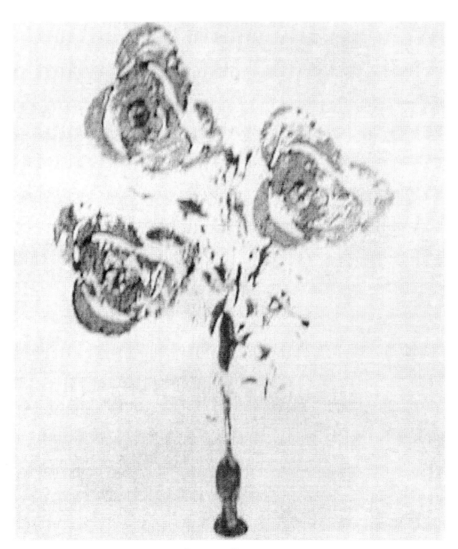

Rosy Rose
To create this type of picture use a celery head and stalk.

• •

Making the Paintings

1. Wash and cut enough fruit and vegetables for your whole class. Be creative—use apples, starfruit, lemons and limes, peppers, potatoes, celery, radishes, pea pods, green onions, mushrooms, etc.
2. Provide tempera paint, and let students use the vegetables however they want to produce their desired images. Dipping the edges of the cut vegetables almost always yields interesting patterns. Some will create floral scenes, while others may create other sorts of images.
3. Encourage the students to name their art.
4. This could be a lead-in or companion art project for studying the food pyramid or about plants.

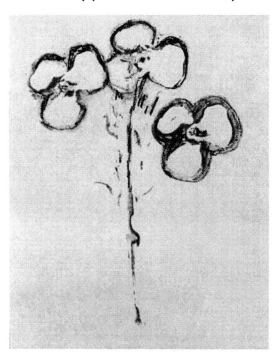 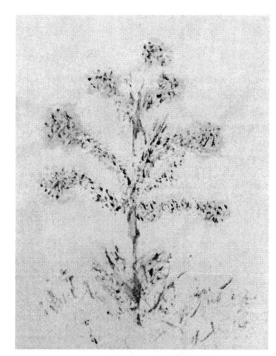

Blue Bouquet
Use a celery stalk to create the stem. Cut off a green pepper at the top to create the flower effect. Use the stem as a handle.

Wild and Wonderful
This illustration is created by using different parts of a green onion.

Very Van Gogh

MATERIALS

1. PICTURE OF VAN GOGH'S *STARRY NIGHT* (CAN BE ACCESSED ON THE SITE NOTED ON NEXT PAGE.)
2. CRAYONS
3. WHITE PAPER
4. WALL TO DISPLAY PICTURES
5. INTERNET

Very Van Gogh

Van Gogh Art Experiment

1. Show the students a copy of Van Gogh's *Starry Night*.
2. As a class, write a story about what is happening in the picture. To start, you might suggest that a person their age walks up to the big tower featured in the painting—then what happens?
3. After the story, ask students if they could paint that picture.
4. Give the students paper and crayons. Then project the *Starry Night* painting where all can see.
5. Allow students adequate time to draw.
6. Encourage students to display their work on a wall in the school that is visible to others.

Additional Ideas

Starry Night was painted when Van Gogh was moving away from the impressionism style of painting to the expressionism style. Discuss these two terms and what they mean in art and painting. For more information about Van Gogh, including, letters, biography, famous paintings, etc., click on the Very Van Gogh link at:

http://www.pittstate.edu/edsc/ssls/fun.html

The above site also features the words to the song "Vincent" by Don McLean. You might want to collaborate with your school music teacher to teach the class this song.

Westward Wagons

MATERIALS

1. TABLES THAT WON'T BE NEEDED ELSEWHERE FOR THE DURATION OF YOUR UNIT
2. LARGE SHEETS OF COLORED PAPER
3. LARGE BOXES TO BE CUT UP FOR WRAPPING SIDES OF TABLES
4. TAPE
5. MAGIC MARKERS
6. STICKS FOR FIRE
7. CLOTHING THAT REPRESENTS 1800s, LIKE LONG DRESSES, OVERALLS, COWBOY HATS.

Westward Wagons

Wagon Train

1. Turn several tables upside down.
2. Put the tables in a large circle.
3. Decorate each as a wagon in a wagon train.
4. Assign various roles to the students as if they were in a wagon train.
5. Bring in pieces of clothing that fit the period like cowboy hats, bonnets, adult dresses that drag on the floor, etc.
6. Create the setting by making a campfire, etc.
7. Ask a local singer and a fiddler to come in and perform.
8. Ask a rancher to talk about the purpose of moving cattle in the cattle drives.
9. Ask the school cooks if they would assist by preparing a sack lunch that represented that time period for the students.
10. Designate a bulletin board and document the journey of the wagon train by mapping out the distance in miles and the names of states or territories covered.
11. For lesson plans related to wagon trains, click on the Westward Wagons link at:
     http://www.pittstate.edu/edsc/ssls/fun.html

Additional Ideas

1. Study the weather and its impact on wagon trains.
2. Study the rules as established by the wagon master.
3. Discuss Native Americans and how they viewed the wagon trains.
4. Discuss the role of the scout.
5. Discuss the role of the cook.

Tips: Novelty Pens •

If you're tired of all of your ink pens disappearing from your desk or workstation, here's a neat and decorative idea.

MATERIALS

- Ink Pens
- Floral Tape (optional)
- Hot Glue and Glue Gun
- Doodads to attach to the top of the pen (flowers, small cars, other small trinkets)

Instructions

Using the hot glue, attach the trinket to the top of the pen.
An optional idea, especially effective if using flowers, is to wrap the barrel of the pen with green floral tape.

Tips: Signage

If you're tired of hearing yourself repeat the answer to the question "Where are the dinosaurs?" here's an idea.

- Place a large plastic or stuffed dinosaur in or near the shelves where the dinosaur books are. The same idea can be carried out throughout high-interest areas.
- Another idea is to find small pictures to describe each section and put the image next to the word on the shelf labels—for instance, pictures of various sports' balls in the sports section.

Tips: "Critter" Control •

If you're tired of all of your "little critters" being out of control, here are a few tips:

Library Media Center Door Line-up
- Using masking tape, put a two-foot strip of tape on the floor at a predetermined spot, inside the media center door.
- Teach the smaller students to line up behind the line, so that they won't block the flow of traffic in and out of the library media center.
- A word of caution: Remove and replace the masking tape once a month to keep the floor from getting sticky.

Training Videos
- Enlist the help of high school students to make humorous "training videos" that show both positive and negative behaviors for the bus, lunchroom, playground, etc.

Tips: Quadrants

If you're tired of students tattling, pushing, hitting, etc., then try this:

- Divide the room into four areas.
- Design each area to have a specific theme, such as ocean, dinosaurs, sports, etc.
- Within each area, create an activity station that one to four students can use at any one time. Examples of this include:

  Quadrant 1
  TV/VCR with four headphones and a variety of short, high-interest, educational videos.
  Quadrant 2
  Plastic dinosaur collection, books, and other dinosaur-related materials.
  Quadrant 3
  Computer station with various educational software available.
  Quadrant 4
  Projects related to a chosen topic.

- Notice that these stations can be changed to focus on the current lessons being taught. For instance, a theme might be bats. In one quadrant put books and manipulative items related to bats. In another, put videos about bats. In the next, students can pull up websites about bats that have already been bookmarked. Finally, students can do a craft project related to bats. By using the quadrants, students are exposed to the materials using various learning styles.

Tips: Die Cutting
Machines

If you're tired of not being able to make your posters anything more interesting than a square or a circular shape, try this:

- Cut out any die-cut shape that you wish to use in a larger size.
- Using an opaque projector, enlarge the shape to the desired size and trace.
- If you don't have access to an opaque projector, copy the shape onto a transparency, and use an overhead projector to enlarge the image instead.
- Another idea is to make your own Big Books, or let your students make Big Books. Trace the enlarged image onto two pieces of card stock and onto as many sheets of paper as needed for story pages. Bind these with staples, yarn, plastic comb binders, etc.

Tips: Bulletin Board Organization

If you're tired of never being able to find your bulletin board ideas from a previous year, try this:

- Create a folder on your computer desktop and store digital pictures of the bulletin boards you create.
- Labeling these by months, themes, or special occasions will help you remember exactly what you did, so that you can either repeat them or avoid doing the same thing twice.
- Create files to store the actual bulletin board materials, and label these identically to the digital images.

Papier-Maché
Paste Recipe ·
·

Ingredients

- 1/2 cup all-purpose flour
- 2 cups cold water
- 2 cups boiling water
- 3 tbsp. sugar

Making the Papier-Mâché Paste

1. Mix the flour and the cold water together.
2. Add the mixture to the boiling water. Leave the mixture on heat, and allow it to return to a boil.
3. Remove the mixture from the heat and mix in the sugar.
4. The mixture will thicken as it cools.

An optional method requiring no heat and less time is to put flour in a bowl and slowly add water, a little at a time, until you have a soupy paste.

To papier-mâché, dip strips of newspaper into the paste. Then, use the coated strips to completely cover your form (a balloon, in most cases). Let dry, and then repeat two or three times for a strong shape.

Pomping:

Cut tissue paper into one-inch square pieces. Wrap each square around the eraser end of a pencil, and dab the end with glue. Using the pencil to hold it down, press the tissue paper firmly onto the papier-mâché. Repeat until the entire surface is covered with the tissue paper.

Castle Patterns

The patterns on the following three pages are used to build the castle in the Can-Do Castle project on page 16. A more complete set of instructions is given there.

Tower Pattern:
1. Make four copies of the pattern.
2. Color/decorate as desired.
3. Cut out shaded areas and glue into a cylinder.

Wall Pattern:
1. Make four copies of the pattern.
2. Color/decorate as desired.
3. Put glue along the left edge (where the Xs are).
4. Glue pages together.
5. Make four folds to make a square.
6. Fold and glue last edge.

Roof Pattern:
1. Make one copy of the pattern.
2. Color/decorate as desired.
3. Cut slits to the middle of the circles, and then tape the circles into a cone shape for the roofs of the towers.

Tower Pattern ·

Wall Pattern

98

Roof Pattern

Magnet Activity Worksheet ·

Name_____ Date_____

Item Tested	Do you think it is magnetic?	Is it magnetic?

How many paper clips do you think the magnet will hold?_____

How many paper clips did it actually hold?_____

Fabric Dragon Face Pattern

fold line

Paper Dragon Face
Pattern

Topic Index

Age Level Index

Age Level Index

All Grades

Meet the Author

Sue Stidham is the director of the Instructional Resource Center at Pittsburg State University. She also serves as the director for the Library Media Specialist Program and as an assistant professor in educational technology. During her twenty-four year educational career, Sue taught English at both the high school and college level, served as a library media specialist in a public school, and now teaches future library media specialists at the university level.

Sue's primary hobby is to get the best quality product for the least amount of money. This hobby led directly to writing this book for teachers and media specialists in their pursuit of teaching excellence on limited budgets.